IMAGES
of America

VERMILION COUNTY

This memorial east of Ridge Farm commemorates the William Henry Harrison Indian treaty of 1809. The treaty with the Potawatomi and Kickapoo Indians opened the way for settlement along the Wabash. This narrow strip of land of the treaty extended to the Vermilion River. Harrison later became the ninth president of the United States, serving from March to April 1841. He died in office, leaving Vice Pres. John Tyler to become the 10th president of the United States. The memorial was erected by the Woman's Club of Ridge Farm, Illinois, in 1927.

On the Cover: Corn wagons line up on East Main Street to wait their turn to unload at the Hoopeston Canning Company. Horses and mules were used to haul corn wagons to the factories. There were no tractors to haul the harvest. The corn was picked by hand, loaded onto corn wagons, and taken to the factory. Some of Hoopeston's famous brands were Stokely USA and Joan of Arc.

IMAGES
of America

VERMILION COUNTY

Carol Johnson Hicks

ARCADIA
PUBLISHING

ISBN 978-1-4671-0497-5

Published by Arcadia Publishing
Charleston, South Carolina

Printed in the United States of America

Library of Congress Control Number: 2019954946

For all general information, please contact Arcadia Publishing:
Telephone 843-853-2070
Fax 843-853-0044
E-mail sales@arcadiapublishing.com
For customer service and orders:
Toll-Free 1-888-313-2665

Visit us on the Internet at www.arcadiapublishing.com

This book is dedicated to my parents, Jay and Doris Johnson, and Grandmas Pearl Johnson and Addie Bostwick, all who encouraged me to write and believed I could do anything I set my mind to do, and to my brothers, Jay Jr. "Shorty" and Mike Johnson, who made life more interesting (mostly) as we grew up. I also dedicate this book to Jean Minick, my historical research mentor. You are greatly missed.

Contents

Acknowledgments

I would like to thank all the people who loaned or gave photographs, histories, and postcards for this book; the Hoopeston Public Library for always being there to help guide me in my research; Tom Sweeney and all his helpers for organizing the Illinois Room so I can find what I need easier; Lynn Magers, Julie Todd, Sara Cast, Darlene Musk, the late Howard Christiansen, Pat Bailey, Linda Rosnett, and Randy Graham for sharing their special photographs and stories; and everyone who allowed me to use a photograph. You are all greatly appreciated. I would also like to include Nancy Thorn and Dennis Morgan, my traveling companions and guides, who helped hunt down towns to photographs, and lastly Alex Houmes for being my backup scanner. You are all greatly appreciated! Thank you to Caitrin Cunningham and the many people at Arcadia for their support and guidance with this project. All images in this book are from my private collection unless otherwise noted.

INTRODUCTION

The counties that developed after Illinois became a state in 1818 changed frequently until 1859, when they were set as they are today.

Vermilion County, established on January 18, 1826, extended from its southern boundary with part of Edgar County to Putnam County and included Champaign and Ford Counties to the west; parts of Cook, Will, Iroquois, and Livingston Counties to the north; and to the Indiana state line on the east. Vermilion County still included Ford County in 1833, when most of the other counties had already evolved from Vermilion; the current boundaries of Vermilion were established in 1859 when Ford County separated.

Among the first residents in the Vermilion County area were the Kickapoo and Potawatomi Indians. Their villages lay at the juncture of the north-south forks of the Vermilion River, near the saline wells. The wells here drew buffalo and other animals to the area, making game plentiful. The saline wells also attracted settlers from the southern and eastern states.

The first person to visit the area, according to some histories, was Joseph Barron, an Indian interpreter for Gen. William Henry Harrison. Barron arrived in 1801, the year after the Indiana Territory was organized. During this time, Illinois was considered part of the Indiana Territory. Although Barron made no move to develop the saline wells, he did see the potential and 20 years later came back to manufacture salt in the Vermilion River area. The actual manufacture of salt, however, did not begin until 1824.

Harrison was appointed secretary of the Northwest Territory in 1798 and was elected delegate of the area in 1799. Two years later, Pres. John Adams named him governor of the Indiana Territory, which he held until 1812. Harrison began negotiations in 1809 with the Kickapoo and Potawatomi tribes to obtain land along the Wabash for settlement. The negotiations proved successful and resulted in the Treaty of Fort Wayne. The three million acres of land purchased for $10,000 was known as the Harrison Purchase and lay partly on a tract of land in Elwood Township. The Women's Club of Ridge Farm placed a boulder in the area to commemorate the Elwood spot in 1927. The Kickapoo and Potawatomi tribes remained in Vermilion County until 1818, when Illinois became a state. Some may have remained after 1818, settling in the area.

Settlers arrived in Vermilion County in 1819, building cabins near the saline springs west of Danville and establishing the settlement of Butler's Point. Johnson's Point, just west of Georgetown, was also established in 1819. Probably smaller villages arose between 1819 and 1826; however, the main ones were Georgetown, founded in 1826; Rossville, originally known as Liggett's Grove and Henpeck, in 1829; Danville, founded in 1827; and Hoopeston, founded in 1871 at the crossroads of two railroads, the Lafayette, Bloomington & Western and the Chicago, Danville & Vincennes. These four cities were, and still are, the largest in Vermilion County, with Danville as the county seat. Butler's Point and Johnson's Point are not in existence today.

Men from the area were called to action during the Winnebago Indian uprising of 1827 after Fort Dearborn in Chicago sent out the alarm that the Winnebago were set to attack for a second time. Gurdon S. Hubbard, fur trader and merchant from Danville, was in Chicago with his merchandise at that time and brought word to Danville of the uprising. He raised a battalion of approximately 50 men to aid Fort Dearborn. The battalion remained at Fort Dearborn for seven or eight days before returning to Danville. The Indians did not attack.

Hubbard, who set up a trading post in Danville, is noted for his travels with furs and merchandise, trading or selling goods to settlers in the area and points north and south. The trail he blazed to Chicago and south, the Hubbard Trail, became the Dixie Highway, known today as Route 1. Many markers showing the original trail can be found along Route 1 in Vermilion County and several other counties to the north and south. In Vermilion County, they are located at Hoopeston, Rossville, south of Rossville on Route 1 near Mann's Chapel, and points south.

A second Indian war, the Black Hawk War of 1832, again saw the Vermilion County militia called to serve. The militia got as far as Naperville when word came from the governor to return home. The Black Hawk War was over. Among the militia at that time was a young man by the name of Lincoln—Abraham Lincoln. He plied his trade as a lawyer in the Danville area and counties around Vermilion and later became the 16th president of the United States in 1860.

The next war in which Vermilion County men played a major role was the Civil War. When Lincoln called for militia men, Vermilion County was among the first to raise companies. The 25th Regiment Illinois Volunteers, the 35th Regiment, 37th Regiment, 73rd Regiment, and the 125th Regiment all served with distinction and honor during the Civil War. The regiments saw battles at Pea Ridge, Corinth, Chickamauga, Kenesaw Mountain, Stone River, Perrysville, and at the fall of Atlanta, to name a few. They were brutal battles with many young Vermilion County men not returning. Many of those who did had health issues later in life.

Vermilion County has fought in all major wars when called upon and will continue to do so in the future to preserve our way of life and our freedoms. This is just a brief history of Vermilion County's early years, but it is not the whole story. There is so much more.

Villages located in Vermilion County today are Allerton, Alvin, Belgium, Bismarck, Catlin, Fairmount, Fithian, Henning, Indianola, Muncie, Oakwood, Potomac, Rankin, Ridge Farm, Sidell, Tilton, and Westville.

Unincorporated communities are Armstrong, Batestown, Cheneyville, Collison, East Lynn, Hartshorn, Hegeler, Hillery, Hope, Jamaica, Jamesburg, Newtown, Reilly, and Olivet.

Settlements that were established but are now extinct include Archie, Blue Grass City, Butler's Point, Burr Oak, Conkeytown, Denmark, Ellis, Franklin, Geneva, Gilbert, Humrick, Johnson's Point, Johnsonville, Kentucky, Munroe, Myersville, Pellsville, Prospect City, Shepherd's Town, Watkins Grove, and Weaver City.

Seven highways (Routes 1, 9, 136, 119 [short eight-mile road], 150, 49, 45) and one interstate (I-74) pass through Vermilion County, making it a crossroads for many travelers and truckers. It is also a pathway for some coast-to-coast runners, walkers, and bikers.

One such coast-to-coast runner, 70-year-old Bjorn Suneson from Stockholm, Sweden, came through Vermilion County April 24, 2019, on his seventh coast-to-coast run. Suneson stopped in Hoopeston, his third overnight pit stop in the town. His other visits were in 2014 and 2018. Suneson stated to his contact in Hoopeston that "all roads lead to Hoopeston." All roads do seem to lead to Vermilion County.

One

Hoopeston

The Willdon Building was constructed in 1905 by J.S. McFerren. The building, named after McFerren's sons William and Donald, first opened with a department store on the bottom floor, second floor, and basement, with offices on the top three floors. Later, the first floor contained the Palmer Bank followed by the City National Bank. The Hoopeston Chamber of Commerce, doctor and lawyer offices, and the office of the Lorraine Theatre group were found in the top four floors. The Willdon Building's five floors make it Hoopeston's only "skyscraper."

Early farmers used mules as well as horses to disc the fields to plant sweet corn and other crops around Hoopeston. This postcard shows teams of four mules used to disc and work the fields, with a scattering of horses in some teams.

Penn Street was one of the earliest roads in Hoopeston. This postcard shows West Penn Street, west of Second Avenue, in what was known as the town of Leeds. Leeds was one of the first villages that made up the three areas of Hoopeston in 1871, each vying to become the main town. The brick streets were paved around 1895.

When the circus came to town and paraded down East Main Street, residents of Hoopeston turned out with excitement. This postcard shows part of the first three blocks east of the railroad junction of East Main Street as the circus travels west down the street. The clock tower is prominent in the foreground, and the early water tower can be seen rising tall in the distance.

The Horse Nail Company, located north of the railroad junction, was established before the 1900s. William Moore, the mayor (1917–1919), as well as H. Trego, Jason A. Cunningham, John I. Hamilton, Charles. N. Cary, and W.W. Todd helped to establish the company, which made nails for horseshoes locally and across the nation. The factory burned to the ground on December 18, 1908.

Decoration Day was celebrated with a parade down East Main Street. The townsfolk dressed up in their best outfits, with women donning special hats for the occasion. Women's organizations took part in the parade, as did members of Hoopeston's Harmon Post 115 Grand Army of the Republic.

The Hoopeston National Bank on the northwest corner of Main and Market Streets was established in June 1909 by I.E. Merritt and Mark R. Koplin. Koplin left in 1922 to work in another bank. The Hoopeston National Bank served as the community's second bank until it burned completely in 1937.

This early postcard shows the Methodist church at East Main and Third Streets. The church came into existence in 1872. Services were held at first in a grocery store on East McCracken Avenue. The brick church was built in 1896 at a cost of $23,000 to house the large congregation.

The Hoopes-Cunningham Mansion was built in 1879–1880 for Thomas Hoopes, namesake and one of the major founders of Hoopeston. At that time, his home was considered the tallest in Hoopeston. It was listed in the National Register of Historic Places on September 11, 1985.

These postcards show the Horse Nail Company prior to and after the fire that destroyed it on December 18, 1908. The business was destroyed completely and eventually torn down. It was located by the north-south railroad on West Thompson Avenue. In 1907, the Horse Nail Company had earned such a worldwide reputation that a business from London, England, proposed the company expand into England.

This postcard shows the McFerren Park boathouse, built in 1915 on the park's four-million-gallon lagoon. Couples or individuals could rent boats for an afternoon outing or take advantage of the pool at the south end. The boathouse was on an island accessible only by a rustic bridge.

The Hoopeston welcome sign was just north of the Main Street entrance on Route 1 in 1984. It was a promotional advertisement touting Hoopeston as the "Sweet Corn Capital of the World." The advertisement was sponsored by the Hoopeston Lion's Club and Jaycees, the Business and Professional Women's Club National Federation, Hubbard Trail Country Club, and the Hoopeston Chamber of Commerce.

This 1910 postcard shows an early home at 404 East Penn Street, at the corner of Third Street in Hoopeston. This home today belongs to the Charles Powell family. In the background and a little to the right is a glimpse of the first water tower.

WORKS OF THE SPRAGUE CANNING MACHINERY COMPANY, Hoopeston, Illinois

The Sprague Canning Machine Company, shown in this 1904 postcard, was located at 103 East Maple Street. Daniel G. Trench and B.P. Crane of New York organized the business in 1892. When Ogden S. Sells bought the factory in 1923, it was renamed the Sprague-Sells Corporation. In 1932, the company was again renamed after the purchase by another corporation and called the Food Machinery Corporation, or FMC. FMC eventually downsized and finally closed its doors on February 3, 2004. The three-block area was destroyed by fire on June 19, 2013, after J & R Tire Recycling bought the building.

This 1909 postcard shows Hoopeston's Main Street looking west from the corner of Market Street. Main was paved with bricks in 1895 from Second Avenue to Fourth Street, no longer a dirt roadway through the downtown area.

North Market Street was the gateway to Hoopeston's Floral Hill Cemetery, which, ironically, is mostly in Iroquois County, except for a small area on the southeast side of the cemetery. This 1910 postcard shows the roadway being expanded to 18 feet wide as brick was laid down North Market Street to the cemetery in the fall of 1910.

This northern view of the Union train depot in 1910 shows the lookout tower on the right along the Central & Eastern Illinois (C&EI) Railroad tracks and the depot. Two rail lines, the Lafayette, Bloomington & Western (Nickle Plate, now defunct) and the Chicago, Danville & Vincennes (now CSX), were built in 1871 and 1872 to form the junction that later became Hoopeston. The depot was razed on July 28, 1982, after sitting idle for several years with city waste, some hazardous, stored in the building.

The Hoopeston Electric Plant was organized in 1891 by J.S. McFerren and A.H. Trego. This postcard shows several employees and the Colean steam engine that was stored at the plant. The Central Illinois Public Service Company bought the plant in 1941, which was later acquired by Ameren Illinois.

The Methodist Episcopal church, shown in this 1911 postcard, was built in 1874 on the corner of Main and Third Streets. This building served the congregation until the present church was built in 1896.

The McFerren Park lagoon bridge was built shortly after the lagoon was established in the early 1900s as a pathway to the boathouse and swimming area for area residents. Gazebos were placed at both ends to enhance the beauty of the log bridge. (Courtesy of Bill Nicholls.)

The Dixie Highway from Hoopeston to the Iroquois County line, shown in this photograph, was completed in 1917 using bricks that covered the roadway, which was 10 feet wide with four-inch concrete shoulders. The roadway was completed in the 1920s. (Courtesy of the Illinois Department of Transportation.)

This postcard shows the Hoopeston Public Library, founded by the Mary Hartwell Catherwood Club, and first located at Hoopeston City Hall on Market and Davis (now Seminary) Streets. The library, at 110 North Fourth Street, first opened in 1898. Later, a new building was constructed in 1904 with a $12,500 donation by Andrew Carnegie. Alba Honeywell, another of the founding fathers of Hoopeston, donated the land on which the library was built. The north addition of the building was added in 1975. The library now houses over 30,000 items, including books, videos, DVDs, audio cassettes, music CDs, computers, Hoopeston newspapers on microfilm, one microfilm on Robert E. Lee, and the Illinois Room, which displays many Hoopeston historical items donated by area residents and businesses.

Honeywell School was the first school built in 1873 on land furnished by Alba Honeywell in the 400 block of East Honeywell Avenue. The school cost $25,000 to build and housed first through 12th grades. In 1927, a new school was built in the 600 block of East Honeywell Avenue for grades one through eight. An open house was held in March 1928, and the school opened in September 1928 for students and faculty. This postcard shows the first school in 1911 with students lined up outside the front door.

This 1891 postcard shows Greer College. John Greer, one of the early settlers and founders, endowed $50,000 to build the college as "a heritage to all young people who are ambitious to rise in the world." Located in the 600 block of West Main Street, the auditorium had a seating capacity of 700 people. In 1914, the high school combined with the college, remaining as both until the college dissolved in 1926.

Maple High School was formed in 1897 when the high school was moved into the building at the corner of South Fourth and Maple Streets. It was first called Maple High School and sometimes Lincoln High School. The school remained a high school until 1914 when it was moved to Greer College. Fire destroyed Maple Grade School on May 30, 1944. The school was not rebuilt until 1949 and opened in December of that year, several years after World War II ended.

This 1917 postcard shows the Hoopeston water works pumping station on West Main Street. The station was established during I.E. Merritt's term as mayor (1913–1917). Mayors William Moore and John A. Heaton improved the wells that supplied the water to the city, increasing the capacity with an additional well, a new reservoir, and two pressure pumps.

The Hoopes Mansion was built by Thomas Hoopes in the late 1890s. After his death in 1893, his niece and her husband, James Cunningham, bought the house during an auction and remodeled it into a more modern home. Charles Dyer, whose wife was the granddaughter of Cunningham, bought the house in 1925 during the Cunningham auction. The Hoopes-Cunningham Mansion was purchased in 1982 by Peter and Peggy Krimbel and was listed in the National Register of Historic Places in 1985.

The McFerren Park pavilion, shown in this 1925 postcard, was built before 1913 by the Chautauqua Foundation for $7,000. It could seat more than 2,000 people and was considered one of the largest meeting places during Hoopeston's early years. It is still used for many functions by the City of Hoopeston and its residents today, especially during one of the high points of the National Sweetcorn Festival—the National Sweetcorn Sweetheart Pageant.

This postcard of the Union Depot shows a train stopping at the station loading and unloading passengers and freight. On the east side of the tracks, the Western Union Telegraph and cable office can be seen on the west side of the Cunningham Hotel.

The American Can Company had its beginning as the Union Can Company and was established between 1881 and 1882. This Hoopeston postcard shows the plant in the early 1900s. Although the company downsized when the canning factories closed in Hoopeston, Silgan Containers purchased the plant and still maintains a presence in Hoopeston today.

This postcard shows the Commercial Club building on the northwest corner of South Market and Penn Streets. It was the joint effort of the Commercial Club and the Masonic Star Lodge No. 709, Ancient Free and Accepted Masons. Each organization had its own quarters inside the building. The building later became home to the city hall and police station after the original city hall and police station burned.

The First United Presbyterian Church was organized in May 1872, holding meetings in McCracken's store. The church in this 1914 postcard was built in 1876 at a cost of $1,500 on the corner of Third and Davis (now Seminary) Streets. Today, a more modern church stands on the corner of Market Street and Honeywell Avenue.

This 1950s photograph shows Baker's Apparel, G.C. Murphy Co. dime store, Coast to Coast hardware, Lester's Drugs, King's Drugs, Spurgeon's clothing store, and Kroger grocery store in the 200 block of East Main Street. Carp's department store, not shown in this photograph, was on the corner of the block at Market Street.

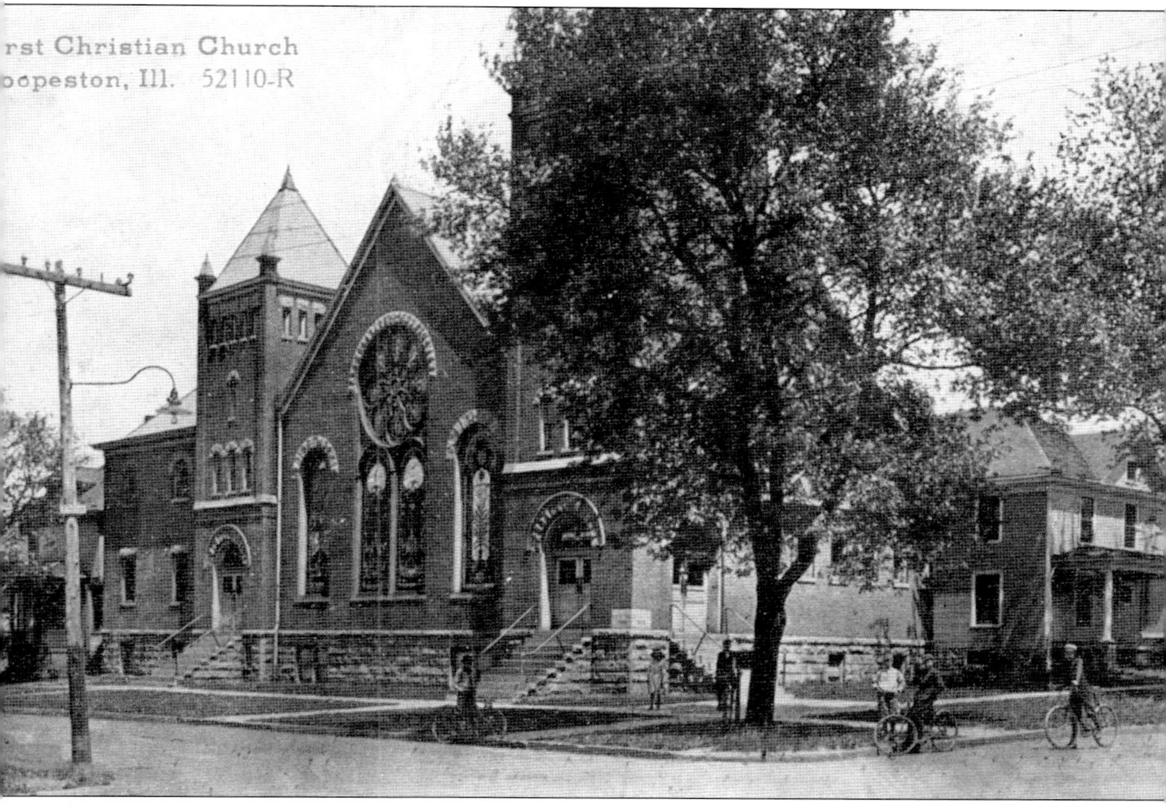

This 1915 postcard shows the First Christian Church on the northeast corner of East Main and Fourth Streets. The church was organized in June 1873. The first building was erected in 1874 at 646 East Honeywell Avenue at a cost of $1,800. In 1885, the church was moved to its present location on the corner of Fourth and Main Streets. It was destroyed on December 18, 1953, with damages estimated at $250,000. It was rebuilt in the same spot.

The Illinois Canning Company, shown in this aerial postcard view, was established in 1875 by S.S. McCall and incorporated in 1877. It was later acquired by Joan of Arc and finally by Pillsbury Foods. When Pillsbury decided to sell the business, employees pooled their money and, in 1995, purchased the business, naming it Hoopeston Foods. The company remained as Hoopeston Foods until Teasdale Quality Foods acquired it in 2012. Teasdale remains a staple in Hoopeston to this day.

This 1907 postcard view is looking east from Bank Street toward the 200 block of East Main Street downtown. The clock tower building is the corner building. The bottom picture shows a complete view of the Union depot.

Faye Mott is pictured in front of the Indian mural in the Lorraine Theatre lobby in downtown Hoopeston. Mott was the 1948 Miss Hoopeston for the National Sweetcorn Festival and the first young lady chosen to reign over the festival after World War II. The National Sweetcorn Festival was canceled during the war and for several years after, from 1941 to 1947. The Hoopeston Jaycees have hosted the festival from 1948 to the present day.

Hoopeston Malleable Iron Works was founded in 1907 and financed by local capital. The company's representatives, S.D. Porter and J.A. Scanland, signed an agreement with the Hoopeston Industrial Committee, consisting of Scott Ingle, J.S. McFerren, J.H. Dyer, John L. Hamilton, and J.W. Heaton, to give $50,000 to insure that two buildings of brick and stone be erected, one at 110 feet by 150 feet and another at 50 feet by 110 feet, as well as a foundry for the manufacturing of malleable iron casting with an additional furnace at a later date. The business would employ 115 men and pay out $75,000 in wages per year. John Deere Corporation acquired the business in January 1977 and it closed around 1982.

The Grab-It-Here store first opened on Saturday, September 22, 1928, at 306 East Main Street, moving to 317 South Market Street around 1955, where it remained until 1979. The owner later sold the location to the Save-A-Lot grocery chain. Save-A-Lot served the community until 1990 when it was sold to the Price-Less chain.

Price Less Foods, formerly Bloyd's, on the corner of Market St. and Washington St., Hoopeston, Illinois in the 1980s.

Price-Less Foods purchased Save-A-Lot in 1990 and opened a store in 1991. Price-Less continued to serve the Hoopeston community until 2014. The store was purchased by a man of Indian descent around 2015, and he opened it as Save-U-More. Save-U-More was only open a few years before the store was closed permanently.

Hoopeston's downtown was a bustling small metropolis in this 1950s photograph. People flooded the streets shopping with family, and cars drove around and around waiting for someone to leave their parking spot. Parking meters were also a part of the town history but are no longer seen in Hoopeston, or in most local communities.

The Hoopeston Post Office was established in October 1871, receiving the first mail from Rossville on December 5 of that year. By January 1872, the post office began receiving mail by train. At that time, the post office was on the corner of Main and Bank Streets in Luken and Mullin's store. The present building at 314 South Market Street was completed at a cost of $10,000 in 1918.

The Hoopeston Canning Company was founded in 1876 by J.S. McFerren, A.H. Trego, and A.T. Catherwood and incorporated in 1911. This 1930 photograph shows vehicles parked in the lot during packing season. The Hoopeston Canning Company was sold to Stokely-Van Camp in 1946 and later to Oconomowoc Canning Company in 1985. Oconomowoc, in order to take advantage of the Stokely name, renamed the company Stokely USA. In late 1997, Chiquita Brands International bought the plant after a boiler exploded and fire destroyed offices and part of one warehouse. It was rebuilt, but the company closed it in 1998.

This late 1940s view of the Illinois Canning Company looking west on First Avenue shows the loading of shucks into corn wagons to be dumped at the cattle pens west and south of Hoopeston. Corn that needed processing was cut off the cobs inside the factory, put into cans, and cooked in cookers. (Courtesy of Gladys Kuntz.)

Downtown Hoopeston is shown in this real-photo postcard of East Penn Street and the railroad tracks, looking northeast. The Hoopeston clock tower and Willdon Building stand out prominently, as does the brick township building in this late 1940s view. (Courtesy of Gladys Kuntz.)

Floral Hill Chapel was built in 1889 by William Silver, ancestor to the Silver Brothers Construction company owners in Hoopeston. Money to erect the chapel was donated by John Greer to have a receiving vault for bodies, which could not be buried during the extreme winter seasons on the prairie. Graves were all dug by hand during this time.

The Lorraine Theatre was the idea of Elijah J. Boorde and his son John Rosslyn in the late 1920s and was brought to fruition in April 1921 when ground was broken for construction. The $100,000 theater opened on March 6, 1922, with enough seating for 800 people. Talking pictures came to the theater in January 1930. In late 1937, the theater was remodeled in an Art Deco style, with the addition of a lighted marque in front, men and women's restrooms, an Indian mural, and a balcony. The Lorraine closed in May 2013, was bought by Fontella Fraley-Krout, and donated to the Save the Lorraine Foundation in December 2013. The theater presently shows live events while still being renovated. The Little Lorraine, formerly known as Lorraine II, opened in 1998 and was renovated in August 2019 to give it a more professional decor.

Hoopeston Routes 1 and 9 were widened and resurfaced in May 1967 by the Illinois Department of Transportation. Service stations during that time, as shown in this photograph, were on all four corners of the highway to take care of traffic in every direction. (Courtesy of the Illinois Department of Transportation.)

Tommy Haas and George Morrison formed a baseball partnership in 1914 and built Haas's ballpark on land owned by Haas west of his South Second Avenue home. The first team the pair sponsored was the Tigers. Morrison dropped out of the partnership about 1920, leaving the field totally in Haas's hands. The team was renamed the Hoopeston Merchants Ball Club, which Haas managed for 56 years. This 1956 photograph by Carl Weber shows a game in progress. (Courtesy of the Hoopeston Historical Society.)

The State of Illinois erected an underpass in 1941 on Route 1 for the New York, Chicago & St. Louis Railroad to prevent the railroad crossing being a hazard to motorists driving south or north on Route 1. The underpass was 15 feet north of the Route 1 and Main Street intersection leading into Hoopeston. After the rail line was abandoned, the trestle was removed in July 1990. (Courtesy of the Illinois Department of Transportation.)

John Greer High School was in session when this 1940s real-photo postcard was taken. Bicycles are parked around the building as well as a couple of 1940s cars belonging to staff members. (Courtesy Gladys Kuntz.)

Young ladies attending John Greer High School in 1931 are playing tennis on the school grounds. The high school was formerly Greer College, which disbanded about 1926. The high school became part of Greer College beginning in 1914.

Spurgeon's was a very popular clothing and dry goods store in the 1940s. Customers shown in this photograph are being waited on by Margaret Wood Unger, far left, and manager Vern Western, far right.

This photograph shows FMC cookers in one of the warehouses of the Hoopeston Canning Company, which was founded in 1876. The company later became best known as Stokeley Van-Camp or Stokely USA. It closed in 1998.

This view of Main Street is looking west from Third Street in this 1938 postcard. It shows the brick streets in downtown Hoopeston and several of the businesses in the 300 block of East Main Street. Sim's Garage, which housed the fire department, and the Lorraine Theatre stand at the corners. Sim's Garage burned down in 1956, taking the structure next door, Wood & Stockers Furniture Store, and many city fire trucks with it.

The TRW, or Western Radio Condenser plant, was completed on June 1, 1953. The Watseka plant contracted with the Hoopeston Industrial Corporation to purchase the land on Route 1 across from McFerren Park for $85,000. The only other plant was in Canada. The plant produced television tuners, push-button tuners for cars, and tuners for military radios. It closed in March 1967. The building was sold to Essex Wire sometime in 1967. Essex Wire opened in 1968 and closed April 1980.

Matthews Grocery at 327 East McCracken Avenue was owned by Bob and Hettie Matthews and was on the south side of North Side Park. It first opened in 1952, according to their son Dick Matthews, and closed about 1972. It was later used as a house and was torn down in 2019. (Courtesy of Pat Bailey.)

This photograph of the 1952 Honeywell Grade School eighth grade graduation class shows Principal Kenneth Hughes, second from right in the second row. Known students are (first row) ? Casner (second from left), Kay Rutledge (third from left), Bob Justice (third from right), and Bill Crose (fourth from right); (second row) Lee Huffman (second from left), Loretta Mitchell (third from left), Rodney Johnson (fifth from left), Vic Vanesse (10th from left), and Tom Mannin (12th from left); (third row, starting at the second person) Orval Kaag (who became the chief of police), Howard Johnson, Glenn Warner, John Bullock, and Dave Matthews. (Courtesy of Hoopeston School District.)

Honeywell Grade School was the first school in Hoopeston, built in 1873 in the 400 block of East Honeywell Avenue and Fourth Street. In 1927, ground was broken for a new modern brick building in the 600 block of East Honeywell Avenue that would house Honeywell students from first to eighth grade. The school opened in the fall of 1928. Honeywell served Hoopeston for 145 years until the end of the 2016–2017 school year, when the doors were closed due to a decrease in the student population. In 2019, the school board decided to demolish the school by August 2020.

The *North Vermilion Chronicle*, launched by Gideon W. Seavey and Dale Wallace in January 1872, was first located on the second story of Moore and Brillhart's hardware store at the northwest corner of Market Street and East Thompson Avenue. It later moved opposite the United Presbyterian Church, then to a frame building that later became Worthens, and in the basement of the First National Bank. This photograph shows the newspaper in the building that presently houses the Hoopeston Multi-Agency on First Avenue. Today, the *Chronicle* is at 308 East Main Street. Other early newspapers were the *Hoopeston Herald*, *Hoopeston News*, *Evening Herald*, *Hoopeston Daily*, *Weekly Chronicle*, *Hoopeston Evening Times*, and the *Chronicle-Herald*.

Corr and Campbell Machinery was a staple in farm implements and farm machinery in early Hoopeston. T.J. Corr and Arthur H. Campbell owned the business on Bank Street. By 1925, however, only Campbell owned the business, and he remodeled it with a larger warehouse that was said to be one of the largest of Hoopeston's semi-industrial concerns.

Ira Owen Kreager American Legion Post No. 384, organized on October 29, 1918, was first located at 114 ½ East Main Street. The post later moved to 205 East Penn Street, housed in the First Apostolic Church, and in December 1948, moved into the stately home of William McFerren at 501 East Penn Street. The Legion unfortunately caught fire in February 1968, destroying the home beyond repair. A modern one-story building was later erected in that location to serve the members today.

Photographed in August 1944, this young man, a tailor by trade, repaired clothing for his fellow prisoners of war at the German prisoner of war camp on the southeast corner of Route 9/Orange Street and South Second Avenue. The small tailor shop was inside the Illinois Canning Company farm building in Hoopeston. (Courtesy of the US Army Signal Corps.)

Two

Danville

The Vermilion County Courthouse in Danville stands on the northeast corner of Vermilion and Main Streets. The first courthouse, built in 1833, was destroyed by fire in 1872 and rebuilt in 1876. When this building was considered too small, it was torn down and a new structure was erected on the same lot and completed in 1917.

Danville's Vermilion Street was a busy one, as this early postcard shows. The roadway has tracks still in use, with a streetcar moving behind the autos on the left.

This little café near East Main Street and Washington Avenue in Danville was made out of two retired horse-drawn streetcars joined together.

In the 1950s, Danville Square on Vermilion Street offered a safe shopping area without the worry of cars. Everyone parked and walked the three-block square to do their shopping, visit restaurants, or take care of other business that brought them downtown.

St. Elizabeth Hospital was established August 1, 1882, and was the only hospital in Vermilion County until Lakeview Hospital was chartered. First housed in a frame building, its original structure was built in 1888; in 1898, the hospital moved to a larger building on Green and Elizabeth Streets and completed additions in 1900 and 1903. The fourth and fifth floors were added in 1929. St. Elizabeth's Catholic sisters and staff cared for 125 patients in 1911. This postcard shows the hospital as it looked in 1942. The hospital is no longer in existence; it closed in 2004 as the Sager campus, and the buildings were demolished in 2006.

The Protestant Hospital Association, later renamed the Lakeview Hospital Association, was chartered in December 1892 by Charles A. Crane, Horace Reed, M.S. Brown, C.H. Little, John A. Griffin, Hiram Woods, C.L. Hawley, and Thomas L. Spellman. The association rented a building on East Fairchild Street, which served as the hospital until a new structure was completed and dedicated on March 12, 1896. The hospital had a 40-bed capacity in 1911. This postcard shows the building as it looked in 1942. Lakeview remains at 812 North Logan Avenue but has undergone many changes to its name, management, and layout. Today, it operates under the name Order of Saint Francis Sacred Heart Medical Center.

A US circuit and district court for the southern district of Illinois in Danville was authorized by Congress in 1890. The Danville Federal Building was erected on the northeast corner of Vermilion and Harrison Streets in September 1909 at a cost of $375,000. The first officers were Judge Francis M. Wright of Urbana, Maj. Daniel Hogler of Mound City as clerk of both the circuit and district courts, Charles P. Hitch of Paris as US marshal, and William E. Trautmann of East St. Louis as US attorney.

Sunset Memorial Park opened in 1932 and was the area's first memorial park–style cemetery. In a memorial park, the headstones lie flat on the ground for easier maintenance. Toward the front of Sunset Memorial Park is the swan lagoon, which hosts two swans, Joe and Nellie, and in the early spring, joined in the spring by several baby swans (cygnets). Sunset Memorial Park has changed since this 1942 postcard, with the addition of a gazebo, several child friendly features, and benches.

Springhill Cemetery was founded in 1864. This 1910 postcard shows the Civil War monument in soldier's circle at Springhill Cemetery. It is the tallest monument in the cemetery, with a bronze soldier on the top at parade rest, and is dedicated to the memory of all soldiers of Vermilion County. The majority buried in the circle are Civil War soldiers, with a few from other wars.

This early-1900s postcard shows people lining the downtown area of North Vermilion Street during a parade. Many are sitting in their buggies or in wagons watching the event.

The Danville Soldiers' Home was opened as a residential facility for disabled veterans in October 1898. This 1910 postcard shows a beautiful landscaped street with a band shell, the residential area, and a chapel. Today, the Veteran's Administration medical center and Danville Area Community College share this area.

This photograph shows the main building at the Danville Soldiers' Home, two miles east of downtown on East Main Street. It served as a residential building for disabled soldiers in 1910. The building was constructed at a cost of $28,277 in 1898 and has since been demolished.

This postcard shows the main administrative building at the Danville veterans' home on East Main Street, probably in the early 1900s.

The Lake Vermilion Dam was built in 1925 to bring a larger supply of water to the Danville area. The dam's 11 gates were replaced in 2019. As a side note, when Lake Vermilion was built, the village of Denmark disappeared forever under its waters.

Ellsworth Park is the oldest of Danville's city parks. It was donated by the Ellsworth Coal Company in 1880 as a place of recreation. This 1910 real-photo postcard shows bathers swimming and enjoying themselves along the beach. The area featured horse racing tracks, and by the 1920s, a nine-hole golf course.

St. James United Methodist Church was organized in 1919 through the merger of the First Methodist Episcopal Church and the Kimber Methodist Episcopal Church. In 1925, Henry Skadden, a church member and architect, remodeled St. James after the French Gothic churches he saw while in the Army during World War II. Located at the corner of Vermilion and Williams Streets, it celebrated 100 years on September 22, 2019.

The Disciples of Christ was originally founded in 1832 by Barton W. Stone. A beautiful brick building was constructed in Danville around 1905 and dedicated in 1906. The official name of the church was changed in 1956 to Central Christian Church. The church at 1101 North Vermilion Street added a preschool in 1955 but closed it on February 15, 2019.

The *Statue of Victory* monument shown on this postcard was dedicated on November 11, 1922, in honor of World War I soldiers and sailors. The statue and Memorial Bridge were the first of their kind to be erected in the county. Built by Chicago sculptor Lorado Taft, the monument was moved in 1955 to its present location just west of the intersection of Gilbert and Main Streets. It was previously in the center of the intersection.

Herb Drews Air Conditioning & Furnace Co.'s Indian, built in 1949, originally had a tomahawk hanging from his belt, as shown in this photograph. In the early 1950s, the tomahawk was stolen by a high school student and returned 30 years later. The family placed it on the Indian; however, the tomahawk was again stolen. Forty years have passed since its removal. According to owner Randy Graham, it is due to be returned. The Indian presently resides at Curtis Orchard in Champaign. (Courtesy of Randy Graham.)

The statue of Indian chief Kesis was loaned to the University of Illinois to be a part of homecoming around 1980 by Herb Drews Air Conditioning & Furnace Co. on the northern edge of Danville, on North Vermilion Street. (Courtesy of Randy Graham.)

Herb Drews Air Conditioning & Furnace Co., with Chief Kesis standing in front, was a familiar sight in the 1950s. (Courtesy of Randy Graham.)

This photograph of 10-year-old Marilyn Ida Drews, daughter of Herb Drews, owner of Drews-Schultz, was taken during the July 4, 1938, parade in Danville. The top part of the Tin Man displayed on the float later stood on legs in front of Herb Drews's heating business on North Vermilion Street. It and Chief Kesis, a memorial to the Kickapoo and Potawatomie Indians who lived in the area, greeted visitors driving into Danville on Route 1. (Courtesy of Randy Graham.)

Bismarck Pleasant View Christian Church first held meetings from 1848 to 1850 in the Nauvoo schoolhouse on West Newell Road in Danville. A new church was built in 1852 near North Bowman Road, near Kentucky, Illinois, just west of Leonard Cemetery, and dedicated in 1853. A fire destroyed part of the church's records; however, it remained in the same location until it moved to Bismarck, Illinois, in 1912, and a new brick church was erected at a cost of $7,000, with part of the original woodwork, pews, and stained-glass windows from the former church placed in the building. In 2001, Pleasant View Christian Church celebrated its 150th anniversary, but as membership declined, the church was forced to close in 2007. The building still stands in Bismarck today. (Courtesy of Nancy Thorn.)

This 1940s postcard shows the Fischer Theater, built in 1884 and known as the Grand Opera House, and the Palace Theater (formerly Lyric Theatre), which opened in 1906. They were both on Vermilion Street in Danville. The Fischer was showing *Miss Tatlock's Millions* while the Palace was showing *Raw Deal*. The theaters closed in 1982. The Palace was demolished in 1995. The Fischer Theater renovation was completed in 2019 with funding provided by Julius Hegeler. It had its grand opening on September 21, 2019, with the Lettermen performing.

The Vermilion County jail was built around 1840 in Danville. It is seen here in 1860. According to legend, the man at center in the long coat and top hat may be Abraham Lincoln. The first sheriff was William Reed.

Movie star Ronald Reagan visited the General Electric plant in Danville around 1955; he is pictured here with an employee at the plant. At the time, Reagan was the host and occasional star of the weekly television show *General Electric Theatre* and spokesman for General Electric.

The administration building for the Danville Veterans Administration (VA) was built on the southeast corner of the VA land by 1900. The 425 acres for the VA campus cost approximately $45,961.25. The original cemetery was a small plot to the east of the two circles on campus. In 1901, a concentric circle was laid out on 30 acres southeast of the original cemetery, and 99 graves were reinterred into the new cemetery.

The mess hall and kitchen was placed in the center of the 12 two-story barracks erected for veterans. Fifteen barracks were supposed to be erected, but by June 1900, only 12 were completed.

Lincoln Park, located at 1000 North Logan Avenue, was established in 1891. The park pavilion was constructed in 1910 for special events. The park concession was built in 1940 as an added enhancement. The historic Lamon House, probably the oldest home in Danville, was built in 1850 by Joseph and Melissa Beckwith Lamon and was moved to Lincoln Park in 1982. Lamon was a cousin of Ward Hill Lamon, Danville attorney and friend and law partner of Abraham Lincoln, who served as Lincoln's bodyguard during the Civil War.

The Sportsmen's Club of Lake Vermilion had its beginning in January 1968 when eight men came together to improve the fishing in Lake Vermilion. Jay Mault, owner of the Vermilion Dam Lodge, and several other resort owners—Bob Mann, Theodore Anderson, Val Cook, Elton Olson, Bill Ellison, John Aronson, and Abel Anderson—set up the club. Early dues were $3.

Lake Franklin, near the Danville Soldiers' Home, may have been known as Lake Clements, a man-made pond used by the soldiers for boating, fishing, and ice-skating. In the fall of 1940, the lake was drained and replaced by a golf course.

According to *Our Holy Family* by Rev. John J. Flattery, the old St. Patrick's Church School on Chester (now Bryan) Avenue was converted into St. Patrick's School in 1881. It operated there until a new school was built on the corner of 502 East Main Street and dedicated in 1891. The school became Holy Family School in 1978 when St. Patrick's and St. Joseph's parishes merged. The school was closed in 2011.

Three

ROSSVILLE

This Rossville postcard shows Attica Street looking west from Chicago Street or the Dixie Highway in the early 1900s. Stores line the two-block area on West Attica Street. Although several buildings remain, many were demolished or torn down to make room for development of homes in the community.

Ervin's Sinclair station in Rossville was on the corner of Benton and Chicago Streets from the 1930s to the 1990s. Its Coca-Cola and S&H Green Stamps signs were common at gas stations.

This early postcard view of Rossville is looking north on Chicago Street and shows mud streets and wooden sidewalks as people walk around shopping. Horse and buggies were the most common mode of transportation at the time. The buildings on the left side of the street burned down in the 2004 fire that destroyed the west side of the block.

Mann's Chapel was built in 1857 in the Mann's Chapel Cemetery, just east of Route 1 on Mann's Chapel Road. The cemetery's first burial took place in August 1839 when the 11-year-old grandson of Samuel Gilbert was buried. The chapel is still in use today for weddings, funerals, and church services.

The Oliver Perry Stufflebeam home was originally the house of Alvan Gilbert and then was owned by the York family. Stufflebeam bought the house from York, but it was destroyed by fire the night of the purchase. Stufflebeam rebuilt the 14-room brick house on the same site, 306 South Chicago Street. Stufflebeam was elected mayor of Rossville twice during his time in Rossville. It was during his 1913 term in office that concrete sidewalks were built, the streets graded, and the brick pavement laid on the roads.

The Presbyterian church was organized on October 12, 1850, in North Fork and then moved to Rossville. The first services were held in the Independent Order of Odd Fellows Hall until a church was built and dedicated in October 1870. Enoch Kingsbury served as the first pastor. Although he was responsible for the church being built, Kingsbury died before it was completed. The 32-foot-by-54-foot building cost $4,660 when built in 1903 and was located on the northwest corner of Chicago Street and Park Place.

Rossville's Hubbard Trail Marker marks Hubbard's Trace, established in 1822 by Gurdon Hubbard. Hubbard was a trapper, trader, and merchant who plied his trade to Chicago and points south. The marker is located at the home that originally belonged to Alvan Gilbert at 306 South Chicago Street. The marker stood beside a curve in the roadway when first built; however, it was moved farther back into the yard next to the home when the curve was removed to straighten the road. Historical markers are also located by McFerren Park in Hoopeston and by Mann's Chapel, south of Rossville.

Four

Rankin

Rankin was established in 1872. The public school is thought to have opened in the late 1880s. This photograph shows the earliest public school. It was deactivated in July 1987, when the students began attending the Hoopeston School District. Rankin paid tuition for each student to attend Hoopeston until 1992, when that district consolidated with the Hoopeston School District. (Courtesy of Lynn Magers.)

The coal tipple in the Rankin train yard was used to load coal into railroad hopper cars for transportation. This tipple could also be used to load rocks. (Courtesy of Lynn Magers.)

The Lake Erie & Western Railroad was built through land owned by W.A. Rankin, a wealthy landowner in the area. Two villages, Rankin and Pellsville (named after W.H. Pells, member of the railroad's board of directors), grew around the railroad, each vying for its own depot. Rankin won, and Pellsville eventually disappeared. (Courtesy of Lynn Magers.)

Hosfield Variety Store in Rankin caught fire on March 17, 1958, destroying the store. The fire was first noticed by fireman Pete Correll, who was sitting across the street in a local tavern and noticed flames in the front of the store. Four trucks of the Rankin Fire Department, with units from East Lynn and Cissna Park and five fire volunteers from Loda, helped contain the fire. (Courtesy of Lynn Magers.)

The Rankin Bank, located on Main Street and Third Avenue, still stands today. It is, however, empty and deteriorating. During its peak, the bank building housed the post office, telephone office, doctor and dentist offices, and a little store. The store kept a coffee pot simmering all the time for postal carriers to enjoy with their lunch. Winter mornings found patrons picking up mail and waiting for news of the area and outside world around the coffee pot. (Courtesy of Lynn Magers.)

The Columbian Hotel was a home away from home for travelers in the early years of Rankin. According to the Rankin centennial book *Stories of a Prairie Town*, the hotel "housed traveling men and women" and served as offices for medical professionals who came on a part-time basis. Lecturers and performers also stayed here, and "railway officials and workers dined here as well as the townspeople." It was razed in 1947; today, the site of the hotel is Dixon Park. (Courtesy of Lynn Magers.)

Brickey's Café was on the same lot where Casey's is today. Brickey's operated during the 1930s and 1940s until the business changed hands, with a man named Hawkins buying the property in 1949. The name was changed to Wel Cum Inn for several years. Casey's later bought the land for its store. (Courtesy of Lynn Magers.)

This photograph shows the Rankin Grade School around 1954. The new high school was built in 1952 on Main Street, relieving the overcrowding of the small school and leaving grades first through eighth there. After consolidation with Hoopeston, both schools were used as living space and later, as they deteriorated, were left to the elements. The old grade school building burned down in June 2019. (Courtesy of Lynn Magers.)

Five

Cheneyville, Catlin, and Ridge Farm

This view of Cheneyville's Main Street looking north from the well shows the village's early homes and businesses. The post office stands just south of the Nickle Plate Railroad. (Courtesy of Darlene Musk.)

John Bergstrom, shown at right, was the owner of Cheneyville's blacksmith shop. In addition to regular blacksmith duties like shoeing horses, he advertised that he also did woodworking for residents. (Courtesy of Darlene Musk.)

This photograph shows the Cheneyville train depot in 1963–1964. The first station agent was Jessie E. Marvin. (Courtesy of Darlene Musk.)

The original school in Cheneyville was built around 1885 at a cost of $3,500. Fire destroyed this first school on February 20, 1902, according to the *Hoopeston Chronicle-Herald*. There was no fire department in Cheneyville, so the building could not be saved. Although the school was only insured for $1,200, in the spring of 1903, the directors proceeded to build a new school on the same lot as the original schoolhouse. The school was used continuously until the end of the 1963–1964 school year, when it was closed. Cheneyville area students were bused to the Hoopeston schools beginning with the 1964–1965 school year. Today, the schoolhouse is the home of David and Darlene Musk. (Courtesy of Darlene Musk.)

This is another view of the schoolhouse at Cheneyville. Jesse E. Marvin and James Smiley were two of the first directors of the school district, and Carrie Owen of Hoopeston was the first teacher. Jarred Lyon was the superintendent of Hoopeston schools when Cheneyville became a part of the school district. (Courtesy of Darlene Musk.)

A mail truck is parked in front of the Reed Bros. welding and repair shop in the 1960s. (Courtesy of Darlene Musk.)

Catlin City Hall is shown in this 1950s photograph. Catlin was founded in 1858. It was previously known as Butler's Point, which was founded in 1820. The first school, which also served as a church, was built there in 1827. The cemetery, God's Acre, is all that remains of Butler's Point. The Potawatomi Trail of Death is known to have traveled through this area in 1838.

The Reilly elevator was built along the C&EI Railroad in 1902 as a spur line to the town of St. Louis. The little town of Reilly sprang up around the elevator and railroad and thrived briefly. Today, there are a few homes around the elevator, but the town itself is no longer in existence. (Courtesy of Nancy Thorn.)

In 1838, Myersville Gristmill and Laury Barn, now located in the Bunker Hill Historic Area of Kennekuk County Park, was originally in the town of Myersville, just west of Bismarck. The C&EI Railroad was built through the area that today is Bismarck, causing Myersville to disappear when most of the businesses moved to be near the railroad. When Zella Brown Laury left the mill and barn to her daughters, they donated it to the Vermilion County Conservation District in the spring of 2000. The barn, the last remaining remnant of Myersville, was completely dismantled and rebuilt at the Bunker Hill Historic Area in December 2001. (Courtesy of Nancy Thorn.)

The Ridge Farm Library was founded in the early 1900s by the Chautauqua Circle. As the library grew, Andrew Carnegie was asked to donate $6,000 to fund it; however, he required that necessary provisions be made to show him that the town could support it. The town voted for a tax that generated $900 a year to support the library, and Carnegie donated the money. Instead of the original requested amount, he donated $9,000. The new library was dedicated on January 14, 1911. The first librarian was Florence Newlin Carmack.

TOWNSHIP HIGH SCHOOL, RIDGEFARM, ILL.

The Ridge Farm High School was established in 1890. It served the area for nearly 100 years until the mid-1980s, when Ridge Farm and Georgetown began discussing consolidation of the two schools. In the summer of 1986, Ridge Farm and Georgetown consolidated into the Georgetown–Ridge Farm School District.

Six

Yankee Point, Newtown, Oakwood, Sidell, Blue Grass City, Jamesburg, Henning, East Lynn, Ellis, and Bunker Hill

Yankee Point School in Love Township was about six miles southeast of Georgetown and three miles north of Ridge Farm. Yankee Point, settled sometime between 1821 and 1823, was named for the large number of settlers from New England. Although the school and village no longer exist, Yankee Point Cemetery does. It is near the site of the old Cumberland Presbyterian Church, which was organized in 1853.

Red Oak School was originally built in 1884, near the community of Newtown. It later burned and was rebuilt in 1917. Red Oak was in use until 1956, when it was closed. The school was relocated in 1989 to the Bunker Hill Historic Area in Kennekuk County Park, where it resides today.

In Oakwood, the Mack & Son Agency Barber Shop was on the corner of South Main and Scott Streets. The building was constructed in 1901 by Elija "Newt" Longstreth. Later, the business went through several barber's hands until Mike Cannon bought it. Verne Swisher, who worked for Cannon, retired in 1975, and Cannon decided to donate the shop to the Bunker Hill Historic Area in 1999.

The Sidell School memorial marks the spot of Sidell's first school, a two-room brick building erected in the 1880s on the west side of Chicago Street. In 1892, a second story was added for the new two-year high school, with an additional year of high school beginning in 1897. Two more rooms were added to the school in 1905, and Sidell's High School District 21 was established in 1912. As the number of students fell, Sidell consolidated with Fairmount, Indianola, and Jamaica to create the Jamaica School District in 1955 with the Jamaica Consolidated High School set in Sidell. Enrollment again dropped, causing Jamaica School District No. 12 to vote in 2014 to consolidate with Catlin and form the Salt Fork School District Unit No. 512 High School and other schools.

Blue Grass City was founded about 1832. When the railroad was built west of its location, it gradually ceased to exist. Originally the village had a tavern, blacksmith shop, store, a post office, and church. The Baptist church was organized in 1852 and was also known as either Hopewell Church or Blue Grass Church. All that remains to mark the approximate spot of the village is the house shown here.

Jamesburg, three miles west of the Bismarck turn-off on Route 1, was a small, thriving village at one time. Today, it is just a group of homes with no business section, grocery stores, or post office. This photograph shows all that remains of the small village.

The present Shiloh Apostolic Church began as the Henning Church of Christ in October 1898, organized under the direction of J.W. Street, a student minister. The following spring, a frame church was erected; in September 1916, the building was destroyed by fire. The church was rebuilt and dedicated in November 1917, serving the Henning community until 1986. Rev. Edward Wilson founded the apostolic group, bought the church building, and moved the Shiloh Apostolic Church into that location on Main Street and Route 136 in Henning.

East Lynn Community Fellowship Hall was erected in 1875 as the First Methodist Church. The church was wooden until it was replaced with the brick building. The church was founded in 1869, before East Lynn was founded in 1872, and services were held until 2011, when it was disbanded. The building was bought by the families of Larry Johnson, Keith Allen, and John Smiley, and is now the independent East Lynn Community Fellowship Church. Services are held on Sunday mornings and Wednesday evenings.

The East Lynn Cross was erected on April 1, 2019, by the East Lynn Community Fellowship Church as a joint project with the East Lynn community. Steiner Farm Drainage moved a rock into place with community and businesses setting and bracing the cross. The war memorial north of the cross was earlier moved to East Lynn Cemetery.

Ellis School opened in 1914 as one of the first rural schools in the area, east of Route 49, with 14 students. Its tenure as a school district lasted until 1918, when it consolidated with the Armstrong School District. Ellis School was officially disbanded in February 1920. Today, the school is used as a home.

Ellis was established in 1902 along a spur of the C&EI Railroad. Its growth spurt did not last long, even though a store and school were developed and a post office opened in 1908 and continued until 1935, when it closed. The only thing left in Ellis today is the elevator and the house that used to be a school.

The Vermilion Chapel, constructed in 1886, is the only original building in the Bunker Hill Historic Area at Kennekuk County Park. Founded in 1863 as a Baptist church, meetings were first held in the Bunker Hill School and members' homes until the church was built. Due to declining membership, the remaining members sold the church to the Vermilion County Conservation District in 1966. The Altrusa Club of Danville restored the chapel as part of its bicentennial project in 1976. The small one-room church features a pump reed organ, podium, decorative stove, oak pews, original glass in the windows, and two separate doors—one for women and one for men.

The Old Print Shop in Bunker Hill Historic Area at Kennekuk County Park is a new building constructed in 2006 through the Julius W. Hegeler II Foundation. It utilized reclaimed woodwork, flooring, doors, and windows from Danville's Douglas School and printing equipment and supplies donated by Faulstich Printing Company, Vernon Light and family, Lloyd Toby, and Ray Wright. Using the printing press, volunteers print souvenir bookmarks or other items for special events held at the historic area.

Seven

Hope, Alvin, Potomac, Indianola, Rankin, Henning, and Others

Hope United Church of Christ chapel sits off Route 49 surrounded by the small village of Hope in Vermilion County. Besides Hope United's own services, the Ogden Christian Church (Disciples of Christ) also holds services at the small church. Hope is the hometown of Mark Van Doren, winner of the 1940 Pulitzer Prize for Poetry, a literary editor for *The Nation*, and a professor of English at Columbia University for 40 years.

The Alvin tornado monument was placed near a little park across from the Alvin Post Office in memory of those residents killed when a tornado devastated the town on Monday, March 16, 1942, destroying the business section of town and 27 homes. Six people died: George Johnson; Jesse Hoover; Dewey Scott; Billy Smith; Henry O'Farrell, who died at Lake View later that night; and Ruth Viles, who died the Saturday following the storm. The only buildings left intact were the grocery store of Ernest Felganhauer; the elevator of George Merritt, which sustained considerable damage; and Alvin Methodist Church.

The Potomac Water Tower stands on East Lynn Road, which runs south of East Lynn into the village of Potomac.

Indianola was founded in 1836 as Chililicothe, renamed in 1844 as Dallas, and finally Indianola. The name changes were due to other post offices having the same name in other counties. The Indianola Bank was founded in 1902 by Richard R. Block and his father, Theodore Block. It sold to William and Anna Cathcart, who ran it until it closed in 1941. The bank became a museum after 1987, formed by the historical society. However, financial woes closed the museum. (Courtesy of Linda Rosnett.)

This photograph, taken around 1910, shows Blaine Willison's Grocery Store at left and Wilbur Gibb's Store and the Opera House at right. The Masonic Hall was above Gibb's Store in Indianola.

Indianola High School was built in 1920–1921 on the east edge of town. It was the home of the Indianola Indians.

The Indianola C&EI train depot was located on North High Street around 1905. Drayman Jack True waits on his wagon for a load of freight to deliver to local businesses.

Greenwood's Service Station in Rankin was run by Rudy Johnson. It is believed it was located on the corner of Route 49 and Route 9, although which corner it was on is unknown. Rankin had service stations on three corners.

The Henning Post Office was first located in the store of J.H. Putman. He was appointed the first postmaster in 1881, remaining in that position until William McKinley was elected president in 1897. Putman also had charge of the American Express Company for both the Illinois Central and C&EI Railroads as well as serving as agent for the Illinois Central Railroad.

This postcard of the Chicago Street School is a mystery. It was originally said to be a Hoopeston school, but there never was one. It is believed to be a Vermilion County school, but no one has yet claimed it.

This Lincoln marker on the Vermilion–Edgar County line on Route 1, south of Ridge Farm, is one of many markers placed around the area of the 8th Judicial Circuit Court in which Abraham Lincoln rode as a lawyer from 1847 to 1859.

About the Organization

The Hoopeston Historical Society, organized on May 18, 1987, was chartered on May 28, 1987. The society was instrumental in publishing Images of America: *Hoopeston* and *Hoopeston: Keeping a Good Thing Growing 1871–1999* with the Hoopeston Chamber of Commerce. Seven members of the historical society also help in the preservation and fundraising for the Lorraine Theatre and are members of the Save the Lorraine Foundation. Contact officers are Tami Goin, president of the Hoopeston Historical Society, at tgoin24@yahoo.com, and Jim Richards, president of the Save the Lorraine Foundation, at richarjester@gmail.com.